This Chicago

City Guide & Journal

BELONGS TO

....

For Evelyn and Tyler - my little city explorers.

1st Edition
Published May 2023
Copyright © 2023 Aileen Choi.
Published by my little city explorer.

ALL RIGHTS RESERVED. No part of this publication may be reproduced, stored in a retrieval system, or transmitted in any form by any means, electronic, mechanical, photocopying, recording or otherwise, except brief extracts for the purpose of review, without the written permission of the author.

Due to the nature of this type of content, all the information in this guidebook is subject to change. We make no warranty about the accuracy or completeness of its content and, to the maximum extent permitted, disclaim all liability from its use.

Image Credits
Key: T = top; M = middle; B = bottom; L = left; R = right
Special thanks to all the attractions that provided images and logos.
28 **Adler Planetarium**; 32 **Chicago's Children Museum**; 34, 35 **Lincoln Park Zoo**; 22ML, 22BL, 22BR, 26BL, 26MR, 26BR **Aileen Choi;**
All other images and design elements **Canva**.

Hi!

This kid's city guide & journal was made just for YOU! Find out all about the FUN things there are to do in the city you are visiting! After learning all about CHICAGO, you can share with your grown-ups what interesting places you want to explore. You can also use this book to journal about your adventures exploring the city.

In this book you will find these sections:

> About Chicago.................................4
> Places to Explore............................13
> Travel Journal.................................44
> Doodle Pages & Souvenirs.........72

Before your visit, ask your grown-ups to check out our website www.mylittlecityexplorer.com (QR code below) for links to attraction websites, restaurant recommendations, and more! They can also leave us a review to let us know how you like this book and any ideas you would like to share.

HAVE FUN EXPLORING!

About Chicago

1. Where in the world is Chicago?

Chicago is a city in Illinois. Illinois is a state located in the United States of America (USA). USA is located in North America.

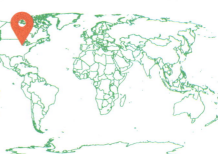

Chicago is located along Lake Michigan which is the world's largest lake that is COMPLETELY within one country.

2. How did Chicago get its name?

The word Chicago is from the French version of the Algonquin language "shikaakwa" which means "striped skunk" or "onion". The area was given this name because there were many wild onions, leeks, and ramps.

The City of Chicago was formed on March 4th, 1837.

3. What nicknames does Chicago have?

Chicago has many nicknames, like: The Windy City, Chi-town, The Second City, The City That Works, Mud City, and City of Big Shoulders. The downtown area of Chicago is called The Loop. After visiting and seeing the city, what nickname would you give it?

My nickname for Chicago: _____

Chicago's Motto
urbs in horto
City in a Garden

4 What is Chicago known for?

Chicago is known for its amazing architecture and the Chicago River that flows through the downtown area.

DID YOU KNOW? The Chicago River flows backwards! The water used to flow from Chicago River into Lake Michigan. However, in the late 1800s it was decided that in order to keep Lake Michigan clean it would be better to reverse the flow.

5 What was the Great Chicago Fire?

The fire destroyed more than 17 thousand buildings and destroyed most of downtown. The fire started in a barn. The reasons the fire got big were because: the city hadn't had rain in months so it was very dry, many buildings were made of wood, and there was another large fire the night before. The fire burned from the evening of Oct. 8, 1871 until Oct. 10 when rain began. The Great Rebuilding began after the fire, leading to the amazing city that Chicago is today.

6 What currency is used in Chicago?

In the United States, currency comes in the form of bills and coins. The smallest bill is the $1 (one dollar) and the largest is $100. The coins are the quarter (0.25 or 25 cents), the dime (0.10), the nickel (0.05), and the penny (0.01).

People of Chicago

1 What do you call people of Chicago?

Chicagoans.

2 How do people get around the city?

Chicagoans have many ways of getting around the city. The L train travels at speeds of up to 55 miles/hour (89 km/hour). A lot of people also get around by walking or biking. There are many bike lanes in the city. An interesting feature of Chicago is that there are multi-leveled streets.

3 What language(s) do Chicagoans speak?

The official language of USA is English.

4 How many Chicagoans are there?

As of 2022, Chicago is home to more than 2.7 million people, it's the city with the third largest population in the USA and the fifth most populated city in North America (after Mexico City, New York City, Los Angeles, and Toronto). Chicago is made up of 77 neighborhoods which are grouped into four areas: The Loop, North side, South side, and West side. In The Loop area, Madison Street divides the city North and South, while State Street divides it East and West.

Places for Popular Chicago Food

Chicago Style Hot Dog

Superdawg
Vienna Beef Factory
Gene & Jude's
Portillo's

Deep Dish Pizza

Lou Malnati's Pizzeria
Giordano's
Peqoud's Pizza
Gino's East
Uno Pizzeria & Grill

 What type of person doesn't like deep dish pizza?

Italian Beef

Portillo's
Johnnie's Beef
Al's #1 Italian Beef
Buona

Jibarito

Jibaritos y Mas
Havana Grill
Jibarito Stop

Answer: a weir-dough.

7

fun & games

What's the Missing Ingredient?

Can you name and draw the missing ingredient for these popular Chicago foods?

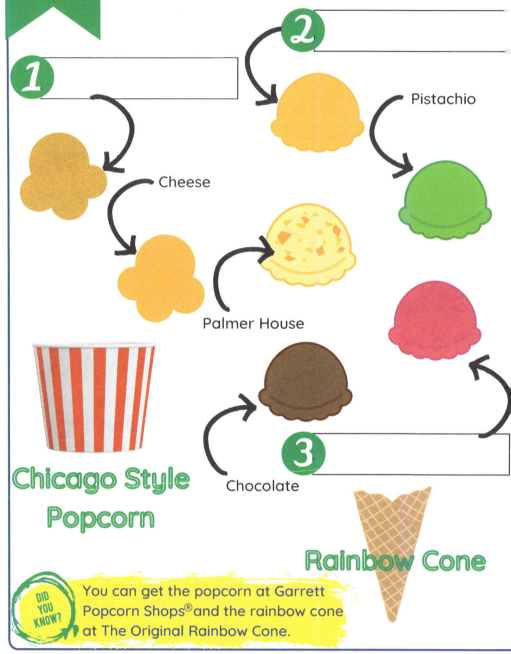

Chicago Style Popcorn

Rainbow Cone

DID YOU KNOW? You can get the popcorn at Garrett Popcorn Shops® and the rainbow cone at The Original Rainbow Cone.

4 What is the final ingredient in the deep dish pizza? Draw and name it.

T

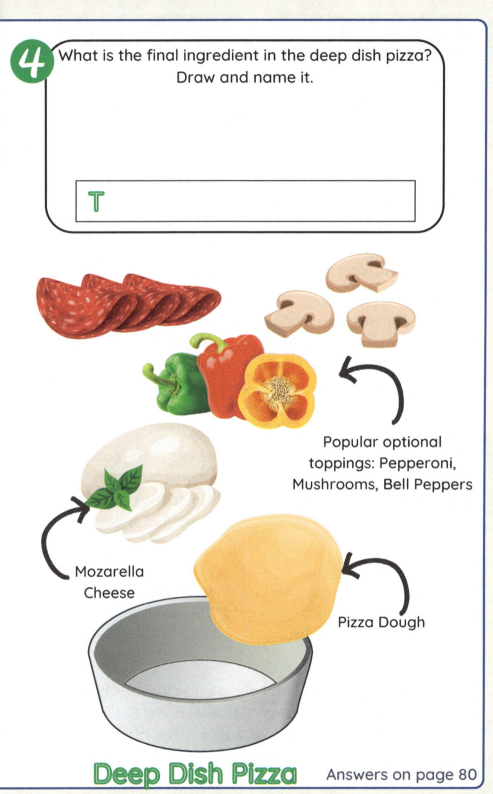

Popular optional toppings: Pepperoni, Mushrooms, Bell Peppers

Mozarella Cheese

Pizza Dough

Deep Dish Pizza   Answers on page 80

Chicago Festivals

Chicago has many fun events throughout the year! Here are a few that you can go to if you are visiting Chicago while they are taking place.

Spring

Mayfest (or Maifest) Chicago
A traditional German celebration for the arrival of spring. At this festival, find lots of yummy German and American foods, music, dancing, and see the crowning of the Maifest Queen!

Midsommarfest
Join in on fun Swedish traditions like dancing around the Maypole, wearing Viking hats, and making floral crowns.

Summer

Chicago Air & Water Show
This spectacular show takes place on the shores of Lake Michigan. See air stunts, parachute teams, demonstrations by the Air/Sea Rescue teams, and more!

Taste of Chicago
Try all of Chicago's delicious food in one place at one of the greatest food festivals in the world. There will be lots of eating, dancing, and music.

Cultural Festivals
There are many cultural festivals taking place in Chicago. Check out: Chinatown Summer Fair, Fiesta del Sol, Taste of Greektown, Taste of Polonia, or Tacos y Tamales.

Fall

Arts in the Dark
See decorative floats, magical puppets, and artistic performances during this fun evening Halloween parade.

Pumpkins
If you like pumpkins, then you might like to visit Chicago during the fall. See the Pier Pumpkin Lights at Navy Pier or go to the Chicago Botanical Garden for the Night of 1,000 Jack-o'-Lanterns.

The Magnificent Mile Lights Festival
A tree lighting ceremony, lots of winter activities, and an amazing parade with over one million lights illuminating Michigan Avenue.

Winter

Winterland at Gallagher Way
Find lots of fun festive activities including a Christkindlmarket Wrigleyville, Santa's workshop, and lots of fun activities inside Wrigley Field - skating, ice bumper cars, and rides!

Christkindlmarket
There's lots to see at this traditional German Christmas Market and lots of yummy foods to try like pretzels, schnitzels, and more.

Polar Adventure Days
This event takes place on Northerly Island. Explore the island, see Husky teams, sit by a bonfire, and join in on other fun winter activities.

States of the United States

Below is a map of the United States of America. There are 50 states.
Can you name them all? Do you live in the USA? Have you visited any of the states?

If you are from USA, color your state **green**.
Can you find Chicago's state, Illinois? Color it **purple**.
Color all the other states you have visited **orange**.

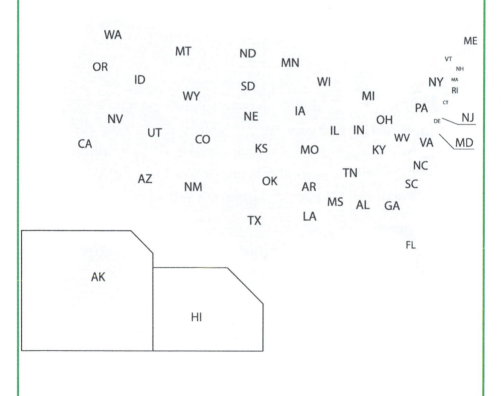

Answers on page 80

Places To Explore

Map of Chicago

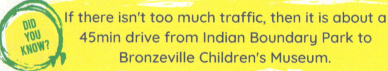

DID YOU KNOW? If there isn't too much traffic, then it is about a 45min drive from Indian Boundary Park to Bronzeville Children's Museum.

Map of Chicago

The Magnificent Mile
Michigan Avenue from Chicago River to Oak Street

The Magnificent Mile is a section of Michigan Avenue that goes from the Chicago River up to Oak Street. There are many places to shop and eat along this street. Inside Water Tower Place, you can find a really large American Girl® Place, along with a LEGO® Store, and the Chicago Sports Museum.

Chicago Riverwalk
Wacker Drive from Lake Michigan West to Lake Street

Along the Chicago River, you will find the Chicago Riverwalk which is 1.25 miles (2km) long. In the warmer months, there's lots of fun water activities. You can join a river boat tour, catch a water taxi, kayak along the river, or jump around the splash pad. There's also a playground.

DID YOU KNOW? The Chicago River gets dyed green every year to celebrate St. Patrick's Day (March 17th).

16

fun & games

Make Your Own Bookmark

Color and cut out your own bookmark. Use these bookmarks to mark the places that you want to visit.

fun & games

Don't forget to decorate the back too!

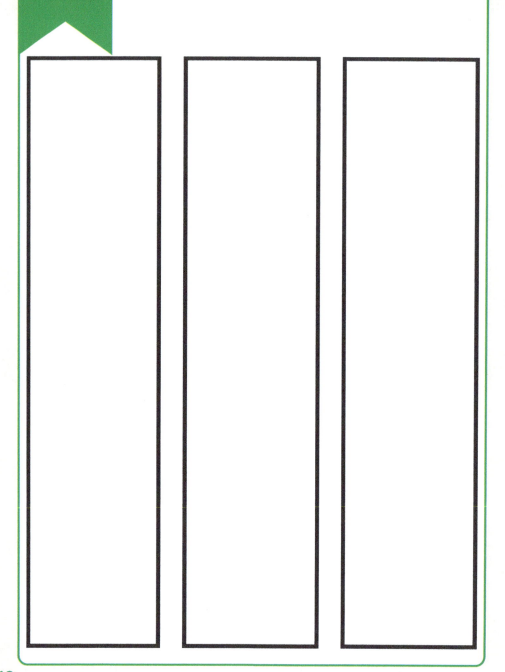

Willis Tower
233 South Wacker Drive, Chicago

At 110-storeys high, it was the world's tallest building for 25 years. It is now the second tallest building in North America. Visit the Skydeck which is the highest observation deck in USA.

Walk out onto The Ledge, a glass box that extends out 4.3 feet (1.3 metres) from the building. You can look straight through the glass down 103 floors. While this might seem scary, you don't need to worry because The Ledge was built to hold up to 10,000lbs (4,500kg). That means it can even hold the weight of a hippopotamus!

DID YOU KNOW? The glass box can retract back into the building! This design makes it easy to clean!

360 Chicago
875 North Michigan Avenue, Chicago

Formerly known as the John Hancock Center, here you can visit the observation deck on the 94th floor and view Chicago from 1,000ft (305m) above. If you are brave and enjoy heights, you can try Chicago's highest thrill ride - TILT. It's just like it sounds! Hang on as you experience tilting over Michigan Avenue.

Grant Park
337 East Randolph Street, Chicago

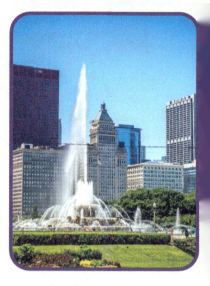

Grant Park is known as "Chicago's Front Yard" and it is where you will find many of Chicago's popular landmarks and attractions. Here you will see one of the world's largest fountains: Buckingham Fountain.

Grant Park is located along the lakefront of Lake Michigan and is home to Millennium Park, Maggie Daley Park, the Art Institute of Chicago, and the Museum Campus.

Design the Perfect Playground

How big would it be? How many slides, monkey bars, see-saws, and swings would it have? Are there any unique structures you would build?

Millennium Park
201 East Randolph Street, Chicago

If you've seen pictures of Chicago, then you've probably seen "The Bean" (official name Cloud Gate). This iconic structure is located inside Millennium Park.

Another popular structure is Crown Fountain which shows videos of Chicagoans spouting water. From May through October, water actually comes spraying out! Other popular areas in the park include Lurie Garden, the McCormick Tribune Plaza & Ice Rink, and Jay Pritzker Pavilion & The Great Lawn.

Maggie Daley Park
337 East Randolph Street, Chicago

Right next to Millennium Park you can find Maggie Daley Park. Here you will find the Play Garden inspired by Alice in Wonderland and Charlie and the Chocolate Factory.

From May to September, activities in the park include: a climbing wall, mini golf, and bungee jumping. There's also a rental counter to rent rollerblades and micro scooters. Starting in November the Ice Skating Ribbon is open.

fun & games

Color These Chicago Related Items

EXPLORE CHICAGO

Shedd Aquarium
1200 South DuSable Lake Shore Drive, Chicago

Abbott Ocenarium is at the centre of Shedd Aquarium. Here you will get to meet dolphins, belugas, sea otters, and more! Learn about the animals during the Animal Spotlights which takes place throughout the day.

Have you ever tried to waddle like a penguin? Go to the Polar Play Zone and you can practice your waddle dressed up as a penguin!

After doing some waddling, get on a kid-sized submarine to explore the Arctic waters.

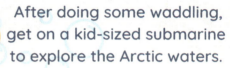

DID YOU KNOW? A group of penguins on land is called a waddle! But, when they are in the water they are called a raft.

At Stingray Touch, you can feel the back of a stingray. How do you think it will feel? Hard? Rough? Smooth? Soft? You might even be able to feed a Stingray!

If you like seeing colorful fishes or coral reefs, then be sure to go to Underwater Beauty, the Wild Reef, and Caribbean Reef where there are plenty of wonderful sea creatures. Can you spot the Flowerhat Jelly, the Queen Angelfish, or the Chocolate Chip Sea Star?

fun & games

Maze

Help the baby otter find it's mommy.

JOKE What does the otter want to be when it grows up?

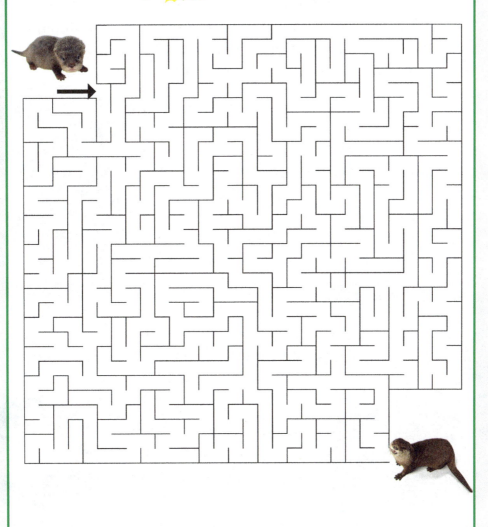

Answer: an otter-naut.

Answers on page 80

25

The Field Museum

1400 South Lake Shore Drive, Chicago

Step onto the main floor of the museum and you will get to meet Máximo, the Titanosaur. *Patagotitan mayorum* is the biggest dinosaur that has been discovered so far! Máximo stretches 122ft (37m) and is 28ft (9m) tall.

Here you can also meet SUE, at 90% complete, SUE is the most complete *Tyrannosaurs rex* in the world. Experience SUE's world, from seeing fossils of other creatures that lived at the same time, to experiencing how SUE would have sounded, smelled like, and how SUE's skin would have felt like.

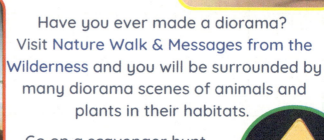

Have you ever made a diorama? Visit Nature Walk & Messages from the Wilderness and you will be surrounded by many diorama scenes of animals and plants in their habitats.

Go on a scavenger hunt - look out for signs that tell you what animals/items to find in each scene!

Have you ever wanted to learn more about Ancient Egyptians? Visit Inside Ancient Egypt to step inside a three-story replica of a mastaba (an ancient Egyptian tomb) and walk through the ancient marketplace.

fun & games

Can You Crack the Code?

The code is written using the Pigpen Cipher - where the letters of the alphabet are replaced with symbols. Can you use the key below to figure out the answer?

Question: Tyrannosaurus Rex is from a Greek word, what does it mean?

Answer:

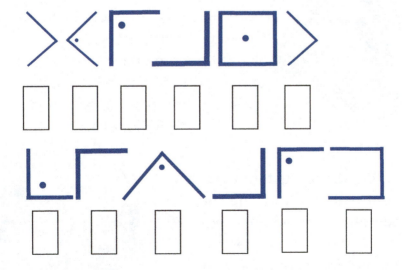

Answers on page 81

1300 South DuSable Lake Shore Drive, Chicago

Do you love outer space? Do you have a favorite planet? Visit the Adler Planetarium where you will get to learn about and explore the universe.

At Mission Moon, you can experience the life of an astronaut. Here you can launch a stomp rocket, build your own filter to save the Apollo 13 mission, and take a look inside a spacecraft!

The USA was the first country to put a person on the moon. The spaceflight was Apollo 11.

Make sure you visit Planet Explorers where you can experience what it's like to become an explorer in outer space. You will get to blast off into space, explore the Space Station, and visit Planet X.

Check out Our Solar System to learn about our eight planets, the sun, and all the other elements that make up the Solar System! Touch a meteorite, a moon rock, and see a rover.

Name the Constellations

Constellations are groups of visible stars. Can you match the names in the box to the constellations below?

Virgo	Ursa Minor	Ursa Major
Taurus	Cassiopeia	

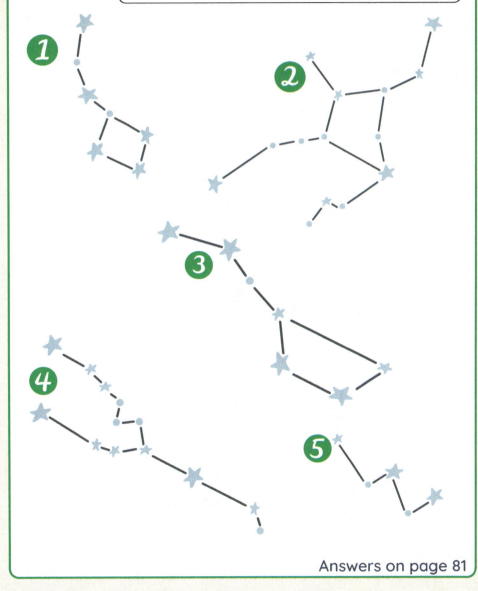

Answers on page 81

Navy Pier
600 East Grand Avenue, Chicago

The pier is 3,300ft (1006m) long and stretches into Lake Michigan.

There are many attractions, places to eat, and things to see.

DID YOU KNOW? The Centennial Wheel was built in honor of Navy Pier's 100th anniversary.

Guess how many gondolas there are on the Ferris wheel: _____

Count them when you go there and see if you are right!

Other attractions located in Pier Park include the Pepsi Wave Swinger, a Carousel, and a drop tower. Navy Pier is also home to lots of shops, places to eat, the Chicago Children's Museum, the Chicago Shakespeare Theater, and more!

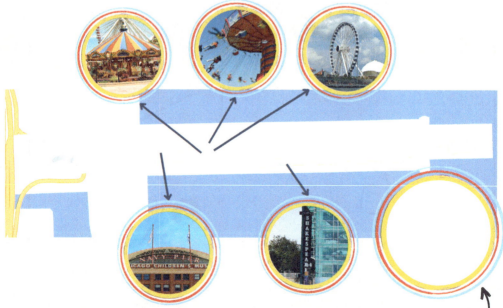

Can you find the U.S.S. Chicago Anchor? Draw it in the blank circle and use an arrow to label where you found it.

fun & games

Draw the Chicago Flag

The Chicago Flag has three white stripes, two blue stripes, and four red stars. Each of the elements of the flag have a special meaning.

North Side

| West Side |

| South Side |

| Lake Michigan and the North Branch of the Chicago River |

| South Branch of the Chicago River and the Canal |

★ Fort Dearborn

★ World's Columbian Exposition of 1893

★ Great Chicago Fire of 1871

★ Century of Progress Exposition of 1933–34

Using the above elements, draw the flag here

Answers on page 81

31

CHICAGO CHILDREN'S MUSEUM

700 East Grand Avenue, Chicago

This is a great place to have fun and play! Become a paleontologist and dig for bones in the excavation pit at the Dinosaur Expedition.

DID YOU KNOW? A paleontologist from Chicago, Paul Sereno, discovered a new type of dinosaur (*Suchomimus*) during an expedition.

Become a firefighter at Play It Safe. You can dress up as a firefighter and when there's a "fire", you can slide down the fireman's pole and drive the truck to put out the "fire".

There's always something going on at the Art Studio and the Tinkering Lab. Make sure to find out what events are taking place during your visit.

If you like heights, then you can explore the Cloud Buster, the Kovler Family Climbing Schooner, and the Treehouse Trails. The Cloud Buster has many levels. Make sure to find your way to the very top which is The Apartment - it's designed to look like a Chicago apartment.

Visit Kids Town to wash a car, change a tire, and shop in a kid-sized grocery store! You can also pretend to drive a CTA (Chicago Transit Authority) bus.

fun & games

How Many Can You Spot?

One day while you are out exploring keep track of how many of these items you see. You can use a tally to keep track of the items.

Remember that:

| = 1 ||||| = 5

Today is: _____

OR

33

LINCOLN PARK ZOO.
FOR WILDLIFE. FOR ALL.
2001 North Clark Street, Chicago

There are nearly 200 unique animal species at this free public zoo. Here you will spot animals like: the American beaver, the snow leopard, the African lion, and more!

Head inside to the Regenstein Small Mammal-Reptile House to visit with slithery snakes like the python, the viper, and the rattlesnake. In this exhibit, you will also get to experience the wildlife across four continents: South America, Africa, Asia, and Australia.

Check out Regenstein Center for African Apes where you can see chimpanzees and gorillas hanging out in the space that was designed for them based on their environmental preferences.

You can view positive reinforcement training for some animals in the zoo - the seals, polar bears, and the gorillas. This involves trainers teaching the animals to participate in their own self-care. Trainers request the animals to perform certain behaviors and reward the animal if the behavior is performed - like a gorilla displaying its teeth.

fun & games

Scavenger Hunt

As you wander through the zoo, see if you can find all of these animals!

☐ Grey Seal

☐ Vulture

☐ Lemur

☐ Chameleon

☐ Camel

☐ Chilean Flamingo

35

Peggy Notebaert Nature Museum
2430 North Cannon Drive, Chicago

In the Judy Istock Butterfly Haven you will find more than 40 butterfly species and 1,000 butterflies - and some birds - flying around! Butterflies are cold-blooded (ectothermic) which means that their bodies don't produce heat. That's why the Butterfly Haven is kept very warm and is a great place to visit if you are looking to get out of the cold!

JOKE
What did the butterfly say when it was being chased?

Do you know how water flows? Do you know if lakes are connected to rivers? Visit RiverWorks to play with water and learn all about how the river system works. Try not to get too wet!

Do you like birds? If you do, then lucky for you, there's over 100 types of replica birds on display at the Birds of Chicago exhibit. How many of these birds have you seen in real life? How many of them can you name?

If you want to see some living animals, then check out the Istock Family Look-In Lab. Here you will see how people care for the animals found in the nature museum.

Answer: I butter fly away.

Chicago Word Search

Words might be forwards, backwards, or diagonal!

```
N W C B P K S S U K Y Y J Y Q A E N R H
W T E I E S I I V C W L T U U T R U Q U
B A Z D U O R W Y J W D K I C T O D I E
N Z V P N M K E T D Y M W Z C R L B Z N
A C P I C Z B K P B J N P B P A P L T I
X U L C A V B Q N A N M L T T C X T K R
G L Y K A C H U A U R S E F P T E J Z I
I D D R Y R A C S N Z C K D T I A A G F
L B U V Y P I R T F I N S J E O R U H L
J M Y Z W S O X C A Q B X Y T N Q I C R
P R R U C L Z L K H C A D F K S M J A R
Y N L M S X R O B Q I H A P K S H J Y I
P J D M C F T U R G A T R E V I R K X W
B V R J U D I Y V V O S E F W R R B C B
B E A K V S H P M G Y T N C S A E P D C
U U L O O P E B H D D W P P T D U Z U X
L W R K L A M U N D A T A K H U M W V F
O G A C I H C I M S S W R V P F R X N U
A P S X J C W Q C S U N K W Q I U E I J
V B G Q Z O J C U H H G S Q J Q O K F Q
```

ARCHITECTURE EXPLORE PIZZA
ATTRACTIONS ILLINOIS RIVER
BEAN LOOP SKYSCRAPERS
CHICAGO MUSEUMS USA
CITY PARKS WINDY

Answers on page 81

Museum of Science & Industry

5700 South DuSable Lake Shore Drive, Chicago

As the largest science center in the Western Hemisphere, here you will find many exhibits to explore including a German submarine, a coal mine, a model railroad, a passenger train, a mirror maze, and so much more.

Visit Genetics and the Baby Chick Hatchery to learn all about DNA and its role in all living things. If you are very lucky, you might get to see a baby chick hatch!

JOKE Where do chickens come from?

Climb aboard a tractor and learn all about the farming life at Farm Tech. Find out how much a cow poops and how that poop is used. You can also try milking a pretend cow.

Have you ever explored a submarine? Here you can climb aboard a National Historic Landmark - the U-505 Submarine. Go down the hatch, check out the galley and "hot bunks", maneuver the periscopes, and find out what it was like being one of the 59 sailors that were on this vessel at the time of its capture.

At Science Storms, you will get to interact with seven natural phenomena: lightning, fire, tornados, avalanches, tsunamis, sunlight and atoms in motion. The best part is you can walk directly into a 40ft (12m) tornado - but, don't worry, it's not as scary as it may seem.

Answer: Chick-ago!

fun & games

American Sign Language (ASL)

Use the ASL alphabet chart to figure out the message. What else can you spell? Try spelling your name!

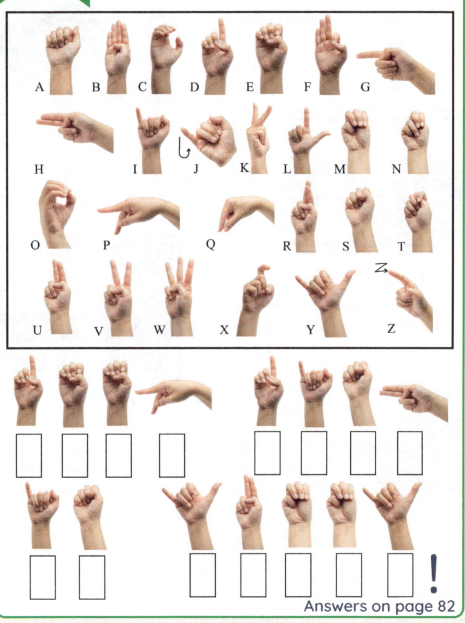

Answers on page 82

Parks & Gardens

Oz Park
If you like The Wizard of Oz, then you can visit Oz Park to see statues of Dorothy, Tin Man, Scarecrow, and Cowardly Lion.

Jackson Park
See the site of the World's Columbian Exposition of 1893. There's also a Japanese Garden where you can see white and pink cherry blossoms in the spring.

Garfield Park Conservatory
Called the "landscape art under glass". See eight indoor display gardens and lots of outdoor themed gardens, a water lily pond, and more!

Indian Boundary Park
Climb a wooden castle playground with slides, bridges, and tunnels, see lots of willow trees, and a pond.

Chicago Botanic Garden
If you enjoy flowers and nature, then take a visit north of Chicago to see the 27 display gardens. From the Rose Garden to the Sensory Garden, you will be surrounded by lovely florals.

The 606
A former railway track converted into a trail. The trail passes through Logan Square, Humboldt Park, Wicker Park, and Bucktown.

Museums

American Writers Museum
If you love to read and write, then this museum is for you. Learn how writers become writers and add a line to the story of the day.

Chicago History Museum
Not only will you get to explore Chicago's history - by learning about the Great Chicago Fire, Lincoln's presidency, and what freedom means - you will also find yourself climbing aboard a L car no. 1, riding a high-wheel bicycle, and becoming a Chicago-style hot dog.

Art Insititute of Chicago
This is one of the oldest and largest art museums in the world with more than 300,000 pieces of art. You can design your own museum tour using the online JourneyMaker before arriving at the museum.

National Museum of Mexican Art
This free museum has Mexican, Latino, and Chicano art and culture. It is the largest Latino cultural institution in the USA.

Bronzeville Children's Museum
The first and only African American children's museum in the USA. Here you can join one hour tours like: You Are What You Eat or African American Inventors Changing Lives,

Brunk Children's Museum of Immigration
Located within the Swedish American Museum, here you can explore Swedish culture and history and learn about the Sweden immigration journey to America. There's also a Viking ship!

Chicago Sports Museum
Explore sports memorabilia, take a skills challenge, and play virtual reality sports.

Wrigley Field
This stadium is home to the Chicago Cubs and was designated as a National Historic Landmark in 2020. Nearby is Gallagher Way which has many events in the summer and winter months.

United Center
Home to the Chicago Bulls and Chicago Blackhawks. Here you can find a statue of Michael Jordan.

Museum of Ice Cream
Love ice cream? Learn about the history of ice cream, eat lots of ice cream, and play in a sprinkle pool.

Sloomoo Institute
A slime museum! Transform into a slime creature, walk over 350 gallons of slime, and design and take home your own 8oz slime.

Museum of Illusions
Check out all of the different optical illusions and rooms that will play tricks on your mind! In this museum, things aren't quite how they seem.

Chicago Architecture Center
Explore a 3D model of Chicago downtown and see replicas of skyscrapers found in Chicago and around the world.

Chicago River Cruise
Experience the wonderful Chicago architecture aboard a boat cruise. Try Wendella or Chicago's First Lady.

Match the Chicago Sports Team

Chicago Cubs & Chicago White Sox — 1

a MLB - Baseball

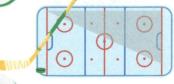

Chicago Fire FC — 2

b NHL - Hockey

Chicago Bulls — 3

c MLS - Soccer

Chicago Blackhawks — 4

d NFL - Football

Chicago Bears — 5

e NBA - Basketball

Answers on page 82

Travel Journal

My Passport

this is me

Name:_____

Age:_____

Height:_____

my fingerprint

My city:_____ and country:_____

My school:_____

My grade: _____

My best friend(s):_____

My favorite color(s): _____

When I grow up,
I want to be:_____

My Travel Details

Traveling to:

This is my _____ time going to Chicago
           (1st, 2nd, etc.)

Travel date: _____ _____ , _____
                (month)   (day)   (year)

Staying for: _____ days and _____ nights.

Traveling with: _____

Traveling by:

My Packing List

#	Item	✔	#	Item	✔
	T-Shirts			Toothbrush Toothpaste	
	Sweaters			Books	
	Shorts			Pencil Case	
	Pants			Toys	
	Pajamas				
	Underwear				
	Socks				
	Hat				
	Shoes				

What else might you need? If you are going in the summer, don't forget your swimwear and sunscreen! In the winter, don't forget your coat and winter accessories!

My Travel Plan

The top three places that I want to visit are:

The foods I look forward to trying are:

I'm feeling   about this trip.

excited   nervous

Don't forget to show this page to your grown-ups and plan your Chicago trip together!

Where I'm Staying

I'm staying at: _____

Inside it looks like this:

Outside it looks like this:

49

I went to _____
(place)

on _____ _____, _____.
    (month)   (day)   (year)

Weather was:
(circle)

I felt:
(circle)

Draw and write about your visit. What was the best part?

50

I went to _____
(place)

on _____ _____, _____.
      (month)   (day)   (year)

Weather was:
(circle)

I felt:
(circle)

Draw and write about your visit. What was the best part?

I went to _____
                    (place)

on _____ _____, _____.
       (month)   (day)   (year)

Weather was:
(circle)

I felt:
(circle)

Draw and write about your visit. What was the best part?

52

I went to _____
(place)

on _____ _____ , _____ .
      (month)   (day)   (year)

Weather was:
(circle)

I felt:
(circle)

Draw and write about your visit. What was the best part?

53

Draw the Chicago Skyline

Get a great view of the Chicago Skyline from Museum Campus or Navy Pier.

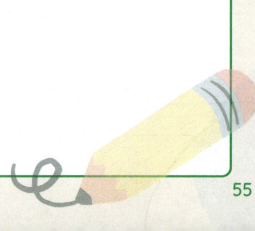

I went to _____
(place)

on _____ _____, _____.
     (month)   (day)   (year)

Weather was:
(circle)

I felt:
(circle)

Draw and write about your visit. What was the best part?

I went to _____
(place)

on _____ _____, _____.
(month) (day) (year)

Weather was:
(circle)

I felt:
(circle)

Draw and write about your visit. What was the best part?

I went to  _____
(place)

on _____ _____, _____.
  (month)   (day)   (year)

Weather was:
(circle)

I felt:
(circle)

Draw and write about your visit. What was the best part?

Sudoku

Fill in the blanks with the missing letters. Make sure the same letter doesn't repeat in a row, a column, or inside the same mini grid.

A   B   C   D   E   F

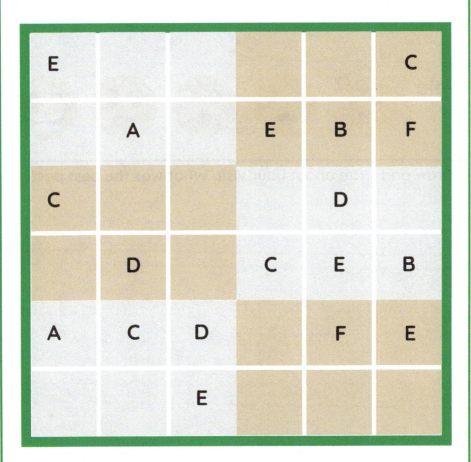

Answers on page 82

I went to

_____
(place)

on _____ _____, _____.
   (month)   (day)   (year)

Weather was:
(circle)

I felt:
(circle)

Draw and write about your visit. What was the best part?

I went to _____
                       (place)

on _____ _____, _____.
        (month)   (day)   (year)

Weather was:
(circle)

I felt:
(circle)

Draw and write about your visit. What was the best part?

61

I went to _____
(place)

on _____ _____, _____.
      (month)   (day)   (year)

Weather was:
(circle)

I felt:
(circle)

Draw and write about your visit. What was the best part?

Color the USA Flag

Can you color in the American flag with red, blue, and white?

Which flag has the highest rating?

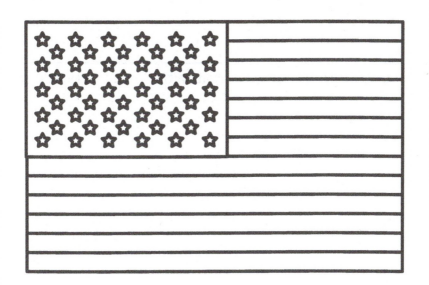

Answer: USA, because it has 50 stars!

Answers on page 82

63

I went to

_____
(place)

on _____ _____, _____.
       (month)   (day)   (year)

Weather was:
(circle)

I felt:
(circle)

Draw and write about your visit. What was the best part?

I went to _____
(place)

on _____ _____, _____.
(month)   (day)   (year)

Weather was:
(circle)

I felt:
(circle)

Draw and write about your visit. What was the best part?

I went to _____

(place)

on _____ _____, _____.
(month)   (day)   (year)

Weather was:
(circle)

I felt:
(circle)

Draw and write about your visit. What was the best part?

fun & games

Chicago Word Hunt

While you are out, see what things you can spot that start with the letters in C-H-I-C-A-G-O.

C _____

H _____

I _____

C _____

A _____

G _____

O _____

I went to  _____
(place)

on _____ _____, _____.
         (month)   (day)   (year)

Weather was:
(circle)

I felt:
(circle)

Draw and write about your visit. What was the best part?

I went to _____
(place)

on _____ _____, _____.
   (month)   (day)   (year)

Weather was:
(circle)

I felt:
(circle)

Draw and write about your visit. What was the best part?

Trip Highlights

The best part of the trip was...

The coolest thing I did was...

The weirdest thing I saw was....

The yummiest thing I ate was...

The thing that surprised me the most was...

Next time I visit Chicago, I want to...

Doodle Pages

Chicago
Chicago
Chicago

Chicago

Chicago

Chicago

Chicago

Souvenirs

Use these pages to glue, tape, or staple: tickets, wristbands, pictures, or other items you would like to keep from your adventures exploring the city.

Fun Day!

Answer Key

Page 8-9 - What's the Missing Ingredient?
1 - Caramel; 2 - Orange Sherbet;
3 - Strawberry;
4 - Tomato Sauce

Page 12 - States of the United States

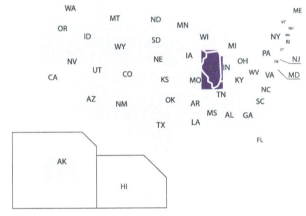

Page 25 - Maze

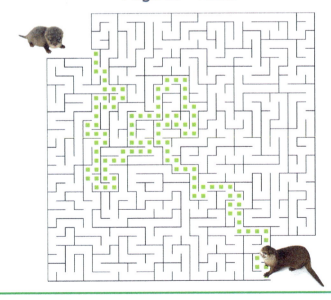

80

Answer Key

Page 27 - Can You Crack the Code?
Answer: TYRANT LIZARD

Page 29 - Name the Constellations
1 - Ursa Major; 2 - Virgo; 3 - Taurus;
4 - Ursa Major; 5 - Cassiopeia

Page 31 - Draw the Chicago Flag

Page 37 - Chicago Word Search

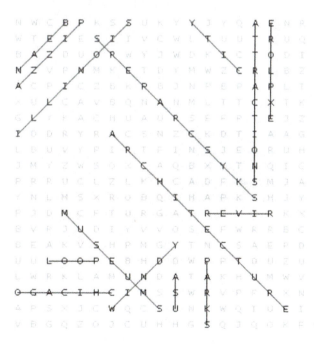

Answer Key

Page 39 - American Sign Language
Message: DEEP DISH IS YUMMY!

Page 43 - Match the Chicago Sports Team
1 - a; 2 - c; 3 - e; 4 - b; 5 - d

Page 59 - Sudoku

E	B	F	D	A	C
D	A	C	E	B	F
C	E	B	F	D	A
F	D	A	C	E	B
A	C	D	B	F	E
B	F	E	A	C	D

Page 63 - Color the USA Flag

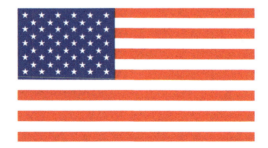

We hope you have a great time in Chicago!

If you liked this book and you are planning a visit to Toronto, Canada, then check out the **Kid's City Guide & Journal - Exploring Toronto - Travel Edition.**

Planning a trip to another city? Let us know so we can create a Kid's City Guide & Journal for that city!

Made in the USA
Monee, IL
13 December 2024